Beautifully stated —
Beautiful Daughter
Fantastic, Mom!

Love,
Mom + Dad

To: _____

From: _____

Love Blooms in a Mother's Heart

a celebration of motherhood

Kathy Davis

simple truths®
Your Destination For Inspiration
an imprint of Sourcebooks, Inc.

Published by Simple Truths, an imprint of Sourcebooks, Inc.
P.O. Box 4410, Naperville, Illinois 60567-4410
(630) 961-3900
Fax: (630) 961-2168
www.sourcebooks.com

Printed and bound in the United States of America.
WOZ 10 9 8 7 6 5 4 3 2 1

In loving memory of my mother,

Ruth Consaley,

whose generous heart, positive outlook,

and gracious approach to life continue

to inspire me and all who knew her.

A Note from the Author

There are as many kinds of mothers in the world as there are flowers in the garden.
And every mother has her own unique, beautiful way of sharing her one-of-a-kind
love with her family. A mother constantly finds new ways to bring her family closer,
to make their lives richer, and to nurture them along life's many paths. Speaking as
a mother, my greatest satisfaction has come from watching my own children navigate
these meandering paths successfully and grow into smart, loving, kind-hearted adults.

Through our mothers, we first learn the meaning of unconditional love. But more than
that, we experience it firsthand...through a gentle touch, a warm smile, even a look
that seems to say so much without saying a word. Her gift of understanding is
probably one of the biggest reasons why we feel so much love for Mom.

Selfless acts of generosity and her unfailing wisdom make a mother who she is, and it can take years before we really see how much she shaped our lives. She teaches us life's greatest lessons, guides us through uncertain times and rainy days, and when the skies turn blue again, says, "I always knew you could do it!" Mothers truly bless our lives with love.

Whether your mom lives just around the corner or is cherished deep in the memories of your heart, may these words of love and wisdom about mothers bring you a little closer to your own.

All my best,

Kathy Davis

A
garden
of love
grows
in a
Mother's
Heart.

Mothers teach us to
live life in

full Bloom.

Look at the world
through a Mother's eyes,
and you'll see a
beautiful
place.

Mother
is another name
for love .

A mother
expresses love to her children
in so many ways...
speaking words of wisdom,
comforting with a warm embrace,
and giving unconditional love.

Mothers
show us beauty
we might
never have
discovered
on our own.

Of all the *hearts*
in the world,
None is as big and kind
and caring
as a
Mother's.

Mothers
create
happy
memories.

A Mother looks for **RainBows** on Rainy days, heals with hugs, and loves with her whole heart.

God could not be everywhere,
and therefore, He invented
mothers.

· Jewish Proverb ·

A mother
is always there
to lend a hand,
to share her love,
to understand.

Mothers
make simple, everyday
occurrences into
special occasions.

A Mother
teaches values,
inspires laughter,
dries tears,
listens intently,
and
loves completely.

Nobody CARES or loves like a Mother.

Mothers always make
time to talk
and always let us know
we're
loved.

A Mother
is the
heart
of the home.

A mother who knows
the value of
kindness, humility,
and integrity
prepares her children
for a future filled
with promise.

mothers
help us
believe in
ourselves.

A mother teaches, guides,
and encourages her children
every step
of the way.

Loving

Kind

Caring

Patient

Thoughtful

Considerate...

Mother

Mothers bless our lives
with
Love.

Mothers let their
children color
outside the lines,
watch them climb
when they could fall,
and allow them to
become who they are
meant to be.

A mother
cares for others,
shares her talents,
and gives from
her heart.

a mother is like
gentle sunshine...
her love warms hearts,
heals hurts...

and helps her children

blossom

and grow.

With her constant love,
a Mother gives her children
the gifts of self-esteem
and security.

The mother's

heart

is the child's schoolroom.

· Henry Ward Beecher ·

A good mother is like a quilt.
She keeps her children warm
but doesn't smother them.

Mothers know the power of a smile,
the strength of a hug, and
the difference a few words
of encouragement can make.

Mother's
life lessons:
fill your life with as much joy
as your heart can hold,
be the first to forgive,
and love as much
as possible.

Mothers
bring
beauty
to everything
around them.

a Mother

helps her children
find their own way
in this world ...

while never losing sight
of where they
came from.

A mother's heart
is a patchwork of love.

·Author Unknown·

54

A mother
understands what
a child does not say.

· Jewish Proverb ·

A Mother offers
a shoulder to lean on
and a smile of support.
She teaches us to be
strong, gracious,
and
CARING.

Mothers know that a

family

is a firm foundation
and being true to ourselves
is the best way
to live.

There's a certain wisdom,
a deep sensitivity, and
an indescribable
capacity to
love ...

that a woman acquires
at the moment she
becomes someone's

mother.

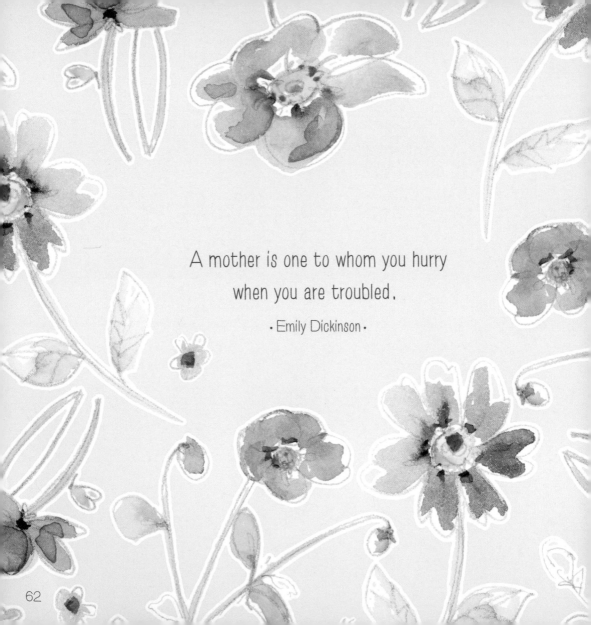

A mother is one to whom you hurry
when you are troubled.

· Emily Dickinson ·

Mothers give us love and support
when we need it most
and deserve it least.

We all need someone
to **believe** in us,
to believe in who we are
and all we can become.
That someone is
a Mother.

Mothers correct without scolding,
teach without preaching...
and give us the **Courage**
to try things on
OUR OWN.

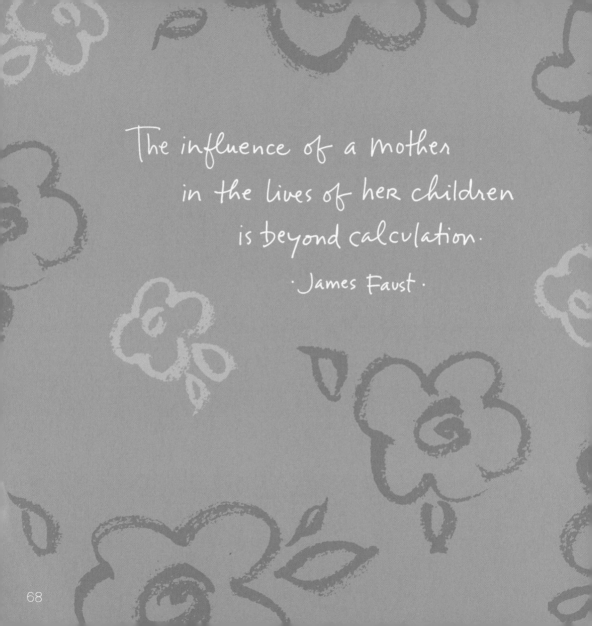

The influence of a mother
in the lives of her children
is beyond calculation.

· James Faust ·

Mothers mean
so much to so many,
but they mean everything
to their
children.

A mother knows
that to love a child
means allowing them
plenty of room
to grow.

Of all
the rights of women,
the greatest is
to be a mother.

· Lin Yutang ·

Mothers
give us the confidence
we need
to believe in ourselves...
and in our potential
to reach our
DREAMS.

a
mother
cheers and encourages,
comforts and guides us.

Mother's love
grows
by giving.

· Charles Lamb ·

a mother's
wisdom and humor
enrich all those around her.
Her insights on life are
the world's best lessons.

a mother's hug
lasts long after
she lets go.

· author Unknown ·

Our understanding of life and love is made
richer by our mother's shining example.

Mothers recognize the simple things that bring others joy
and cheerfully give without expecting anything in return.

A
Mother
holds her
children's hands
for a while, but
their hearts forever.

· Author Unknown ·

How beautifully everything
is arranged by
Nature...

as soon as a child enters the world,
it finds a mother ready to
take care of it.

·Jules Michelet·

Mother planted the seeds
and watered with care,
weeded as needed,
did more than her share.

Her family has
bloomed with
a love that is rare...
she's nurtured them all with
her warm, loving care.

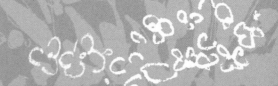

A mother helps
her children find their

wings

and become who
they are meant to be.

Being a mother
     means that your heart is
          no longer yours;
          it wanders wherever
               your children do.

· Author Unknown ·

a Mother teaches us
that manners matter,
hard work pays off,
and *kindness*
is the best gift you
can offer.

Mothers can look
    through a child's eyes
        and see tomorrow.
                · Reed Markham ·

There just aren't enough
words
to tell a Mother
how much we appreciate
her love and support.

Mothers

know how
we feel without even asking,
kiss away the hurts,
chase away the clouds,
and celebrate the
smallest
victories.

We find comfort
in a
mother's touch
and warmth
in her smile.

A mother's love
teaches us to
be patient,
to care about others,
and to help
those in need.

Mothers applaud
all of our
achievements,
no matter
how small.

all the

Love

we come to know in life
springs from the love
we knew as children.

A mother offers guidance
but lets us find our own answers,
discover our own truths,
and **grow**
into our own
unique selves.

There is
no such thing
as a nonworking

mother.

From a mother,
we learn so much
about life, love,
and all the things
that matter most.

Mothers can
help us GROW
by
pointing us
in the Right direction,
then letting us
find our way.

When we think about the people
who truly make a difference,
who care deeply about others,
who give generously
of themselves...

we always think of our

mothers.

a Mother's Love

is the one thing
we know we can always count on,
one thing we keep safe
inside our
hearts.

Motherhood:

all love begins
and ends there.

·Robert Browning·

About the Author

Embracing her lifelong dream for a career with creative freedom, Kathy Davis launched her company in 1990. Today, the former teacher turned artist and entrepreneur manages a growing staff and an extensive portfolio of nearly 40,000 images, acting as chief visionary of the company that bears her name. She is one of America's leading social expression designers.

With her colorful art and inspiring messages on the products she creates in the gift, home decor, paper partyware, fashion accessories, craft, and social expressions industries, she touches more than 70 million consumers worldwide each year.

She is also the author of multiple books, including *Scatter Joy — Create a Life You Love* and *Simple Secrets: 7 Principles to Inspire Success.*

Kathy's brand promise to "Scatter Joy: Joy through Art, Joy through Living, Joy through Giving" permeates all of her designs. Her brand promise is also expressed through her company's charitable giving efforts and support of the arts. Ultimately, her dream is to create a Scatter Joy Center for the Arts.

Kathy's work reflects her lifestyle and the things that inspire her life as a mother, wife, and career woman. Her love of nature, understanding of people, and desire to give back to the world are driving forces in her creative process. For more about Kathy and her studio, visit www.kathydavis.com.

If you have enjoyed this book, we invite you to check out our entire collection of gift books, with free inspirational movies, at www.simpletruths.com. You'll discover it's a great way to inspire friends and family, or to thank your best customers and employees.

For more information, please visit us at:

www.simpletruths.com

Or call us toll-free... **800-900-3427**